STAR WARS

ROGUE ONE ™

SECRET MISSION

Written by Jason Fry

Penguin
Random
House

Project Editor Shari Last
Senior Editor Emma Grange
Designer Chris Gould
Pre-production Producer Marc Staples
Senior Producers Alex Bell, Mary Slater
Managing Editor Sadie Smith
Managing Art Editor Ron Stobbart
Art Director Lisa Lanzarini
Publisher Julie Ferris
Publishing Director Simon Beecroft

For Lucasfilm
Editorial Assistant Samantha Holland
Image Unit Newell Todd, Gabrielle Levenson,
Erik Sanchez, Bryce Pinkos, Tim Mapp
Story Group Pablo Hidalgo, Leland Chee, Matt Martin
Creative Director of Publishing Michael Siglain

First American Edition, 2016
Published in the United States by DK Publishing
345 Hudson Street, New York, New York 10014

Page design copyright © 2016 Dorling Kindersley Limited
DK, a Division of Penguin Random House LLC

16 17 18 19 10 9 8 7 6 5 4 3 2 1
001–288040–Dec/16

© AND TM 2016 LUCASFILM LTD.

A catalog record for this book is available from the Library of Congress.

ISBN 978-1-4654-5265-8 (Hardback)
ISBN 978-1-4654-5264-1 (Paperback)

DK books are available at special discounts when purchased in bulk for
sales promotions, premiums, fund-raising, or educational use. For details, contact:
DK Publishing Special Markets, 345 Hudson Street, New York, New York 10014
SpecialSales@dk.com

Printed and bound in the USA

A WORLD OF IDEAS:
SEE ALL THERE IS TO KNOW

www.dk.com
www.starwars.com

Contents

4   A Galaxy Far, Far Away
6   Key Planets
8   The Empire
14 Timeline
22 Ultimate Weapon
24 The Rebels
36 Rogue One Team
38 Meet the Team
46 K-2SO Specifications
56 Imperial Military
70 Scale of the Empire
72 Rebel Military
76 Mission Report
90 Quiz
92 Glossary
94 Guide for Parents
96 Index

A Galaxy Far, Far Away

The evil Empire rules the galaxy, opposed only by a few groups of rebels fighting for freedom. A generation ago, things were different. There was no Empire. The galaxy was governed by a democratic Republic and kept safe by heroic warriors known as Jedi Knights.

But then the Republic was drawn into a terrible conflict called the Clone Wars. Supreme Chancellor Palpatine, the Republic's leader, betrayed his people. When the war ended,

Palpatine's soldiers destroyed the Jedi,
and Palpatine declared himself Emperor.

Many welcomed the new Galactic Empire
to their planets. Imperial soldiers brought law
and order where often there had been none.
Those who questioned the Empire, however,
were dragged off to prison—or disappeared.

A few brave rebels fought to resist Palpatine.
The Empire responded by secretly building the
Death Star—a battle station with enough
firepower to destroy a planet.

Imperial troopers patrol the occupied moon Jedha,
ensuring no rebels interfere with the Empire's business.

KEY PLANETS

The Empire rules millions of planets, from the thickly populated Core of the galaxy to the sparsely settled Outer Rim. Rebel forces have dared to fight back on a few of these worlds, in the hope that a major victory will turn a spark of rebellion into a flame.

LAH'MU
Lah'mu is a little-known world inhabited by a few farmers. Imperial scientist Galen Erso fled to Lah'mu with his family, but the Empire's deadly agents tracked him down and forced him to continue his work on the Death Star.

YAVIN 4
A jungle-covered moon, Yavin 4 orbits a large planet, Yavin, in the Outer Rim. A massive stone temple on the moon conceals a secret rebel base, one of the Rebellion's most important hidden fortresses.

JEDHA

A chilly desert moon on the edge of the known galaxy, Jedha is the home of the ancient Temple of the Kyber. It is also the location of a base used by Saw Gerrera's group of rebel fighters.

EADU

A world of steep cliffs and rock faces, Eadu is controlled by the Empire. Here, Galen Erso and Director Krennic's team of scientists develop the pioneering technology they need to build a horrifying new superweapon, the Death Star.

SCARIF

A beautiful, tropical planet, Scarif hides the greatest secret in the galaxy: the blueprints for the dreaded Death Star.

The Empire

The vast Empire is ruled by one man: Emperor Palpatine. Palpatine is a villain intent on gaining complete control over the galaxy. As Emperor, he commands the Imperial starfleet and its massive armies. He sends legions of stormtroopers to planets far and wide, enforcing Imperial law. His patrols search for groups of rebels who dare to fight back. Most terrifying of all is the Empire's latest project: construction of a top-secret battle station, known as the Death Star. The Death Star has the power to destroy an entire planet. Palpatine is certain that this threat will crush any opposition to his rule once and for all.

The Death Star's immense size cannot fail to terrify the Empire's enemies.

Orson Krennic is an ambitious officer, eager to impress the Emperor.

Emperor Palpatine's military leaders are ruthless and cruel, just like him. They include Grand Moff Tarkin, governor of the galaxy's Outer Rim Territories, and Orson Krennic, director of the Death Star project.

Palpatine is rarely seen these days, but everyone fears Darth Vader, the armored warrior who acts as the Emperor's second-in-command.

A towering figure in a black cloak and armor, Darth Vader is a mysterious servant of the Emperor. His mere presence is enough to leave battle-hardened soldiers shaking with fear.

Imperial officers still discuss where Darth Vader came from, with wild rumors making the rounds. No one in the Imperial army has ever seen Darth Vader without his helmet and mask, so his identity remains a secret.

Vader is respected as a powerful warrior. He is as deadly during one-to-one combat as he is piloting an Imperial starfighter. Vader has destroyed pirate nests, rebel outposts, Jedi fugitives, and Imperial traitors.

With the Death Star nearing completion after many years of work, Vader is determined to see the battle station operational. This is his master's wish, and Vader will not allow anyone—whether rebel warriors or Imperial traitors—to prevent it from being carried out.

Vader oversees the Death Star project,
ensuring everything runs smoothly.

Orson Krennic is the Empire's Director of Advanced Weapons Research. He leads the Death Star project—and is determined to prove himself to the Emperor. Krennic supervises the Imperial scientists, including his former friend Galen Erso, as they invent new systems and solve many technological puzzles that will be put to use in the Death Star.

Like his rival Grand Moff Tarkin, Krennic believes that giving the Empire absolute power will bring peace to the galaxy. It doesn't bother Krennic that "peace" will mean that the galaxy's people are too afraid to resist. When chief Death Star scientist Galen Erso eventually realized what all his scientific research would be used for, he fled Imperial service.

Krennic is in command of elite black-armored stormtroopers known as death troopers, who tracked Erso down and recaptured him. Erso is now a virtual prisoner in Krennic's lab on the planet Eadu. Krennic is not sorry about how he has treated his former friend, or any of the other scientists. He believes that one day his ruthless methods will be seen as worth the cost.

TIMELINE

NOTE: Dates use the abbreviation BR1 (Before Rogue One)

The origins of the Rogue One mission date back many years: friendships are made and broken, villains rise and fall, and secret plans are set in motion. What will be the fate of the galaxy?

22 BR1–19 BR1: CLONE WARS

Three years of war end with the destruction of the Jedi Order. The Republic's Chancellor Palpatine declares himself Galactic Emperor.

36 BR1: KRENNIC MEETS ERSO

Orson Krennic and Galen Erso meet as students in the Brentaal Futures Program. Impressed by Erso's intelligence, Krennic befriends him.

20 BR1: DEATH STAR CONSTRUCTION BEGINS

The Empire begins building a new superweapon over the planet Geonosis.

22 BR1: JYN IS BORN

A daughter, Jyn, is born to Galen and Lyra Erso on the planet Vallt.

13 BR1: JYN'S ESCAPE

The Ersos are in hiding on the planet Lah'mu when Krennic arrives to capture Galen. Jyn escapes and is rescued by Saw Gerrera.

10 BR1: SCARIF BASE ESTABLISHED

Construction of the Death Star moves to the planet Scarif. The Empire turns the tropical world into a fortress protected by many troops and starships.

19 BR1: THE RISE OF VADER

Former Jedi Knight Anakin Skywalker turns to the dark side and is reborn as the warrior Darth Vader. He is the Emperor's most feared servant.

0 BR1: JOINING THE REBELLION

Jyn is freed by the rebels and recruited to join their fight against the Empire.

Galen Erso is the most brilliant scientist working under Orson Krennic in the Empire's Advanced Weapons Research division. Without Galen, the Empire would be unable to make the Death Star operational.

But Galen isn't working on the battle station of his own free will. He ran away when he realized what Krennic was building. Hiding on the remote planet Lah'mu with his wife Lyra and their daughter Jyn, Galen hoped he would be able to live in peace, but Krennic found him.

Krennic's death troopers dragged Galen off to Eadu to resume his work on the Death Star. Only young Jyn escaped.

Years later, Galen was desperate to prevent the Death Star from becoming operational, so he persuaded an Imperial pilot, Bodhi Rook, to defect. He sent Bodhi to find Saw Gerrera, an old friend of Galen's. Galen asked Bodhi to deliver a message to Saw, warning the rebels about the battle station.

Jyn and Lyra try to escape from the death troopers in the wilds of Lah'mu.

The scientists working on the Death Star are some of the most gifted minds in the galaxy. This is fortunate for Director Krennic, as they're being asked to solve very complex problems. The battle station is believed to be the most complicated construction project ever attempted: A massive machine the size of a moon, with enormous engines that can move it through hyperspace. It also has a weapon more powerful than anything in galactic history.

Ames
Uravan

Rasett
Milio

Vlex
Onopin

Galen Erso and the scientists work on the rainy planet Eadu.

Some of Krennic's scientists have been at work on the battle station for nearly 20 years. The massive project has been divided into pieces, with most scientists working in a single area, such as energy enrichment or shield generation.

The most important researcher by far is Galen Erso, an expert in kyber crystals and their properties. Erso was the one who figured out that aligning many crystals could amplify their energy tremendously, especially when this energy was focused into a single, powerful beam. The Death Star's superlaser dish generates eight such beams, which are then combined by tractor beams into a single, devastating blast of energy.

The Death Star is the Empire's ultimate achievement, an armored battle station the size of a small moon. Its main weapon, a superlaser dish, dominates the top half of the battle station, looking like a grim mechanical eye. The weapon focuses many arrays of kyber crystals into a powerful superlaser, which has enough power to destroy an entire planet.

The Death Star began construction around 20 years ago. Overseen by Grand Moff Tarkin and Orson Krennic on the Emperor's orders, the project has been the Empire's greatest secret.

Death Star troopers at the controls of the battle station.

It has been incredibly expensive and required the invention of brand new technology. Much of this technology has been developed in absolute secrecy by scientists such as Galen Erso.

To Imperial officers, such as Tarkin and Krennic, the Death Star is a technological terror meant to ensure peace. They believe that once its destructive power has been demonstrated, all opposition to the Empire will come to an end.

After all these years of secrecy, the Death Star is almost complete. The Empire is ready to unveil its greatest weapon with the testing of its superlaser!

Thermal exhaust ports—
just two meters wide.

Precisely aligned kyber
crystals focus laser energy.

Equatorial trench
dotted with
docking bays.

Hyperdrive
combines thrust
from 123 field
generators.

Quadanium hull
protects Death
Star's interior.

Crew levels are set just
beneath outer hull.

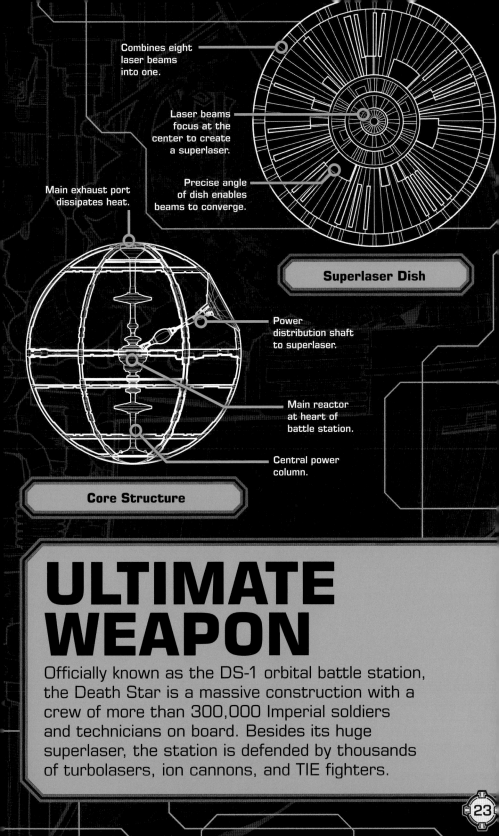

Combines eight
laser beams
into one.

Laser beams
focus at the
center to create
a superlaser.

Main exhaust port
dissipates heat.

Precise angle
of dish enables
beams to converge.

Superlaser Dish

Power
distribution shaft
to superlaser.

Main reactor
at heart of
battle station.

Central power
column.

Core Structure

ULTIMATE WEAPON

Officially known as the DS-1 orbital battle station,
the Death Star is a massive construction with a
crew of more than 300,000 Imperial soldiers
and technicians on board. Besides its huge
superlaser, the station is defended by thousands
of turbolasers, ion cannons, and TIE fighters.

The Rebels

The rebel movement is made up of small groups of fighters, all intent on destroying the Empire.

Each group operates independently of one another. This works as a safety measure: one rebel group cannot give away the secrets of the others.

However, the reason there are many rebel groups has nothing to do with safety! The rebels do not all agree with each other. They cannot decide on the best way to take on the Empire. Should they negotiate with the Empire or attack without delay?

Tensions often rise when various rebel leaders disagree.

With so many different opinions, the rebels are disorganized and ineffective. It is up to Mon Mothma, the rebel leader, to help the various groups cooperate with each other. Mon Mothma works hard to smooth over the differences among her own top officers, but it is not always easy.

One thing all the rebels do agree on: rumors of an upcoming imperial weapons test mean that the galaxy may be about to face a new threat. It is vital to find out more. Immediately!

Mon Mothma

The Empire is already extremely dangerous, dominating the galaxy with its warships and stormtroopers. How can the rebels keep fighting against a weapon that's powerful enough to destroy a planet?

Rebel Intelligence agent Cassian Andor brings some vital information to the rebel leaders. A spy had informed Cassian that an Imperial pilot named Bodhi Rook had defected from the Empire. Bodhi made contact with a rebel militant named Saw Gerrera on the moon Jedha.

Cassian Andor

According to the spy, Bodhi brought a message from Imperial scientist Galen Erso.

Rebel Intelligence discovers that Galen Erso has a daughter, Jyn—a former soldier of Saw's who had turned to a life of crime and was now captive in an Imperial prison. Rebel soldiers are sent to free Jyn and bring her to the rebel base on Yavin 4, hopeful she can lead them to Saw.

Jyn has been on her own for a while and she is naturally distrustful of others. She is surprised when the rebel soldiers bring her straight to the command center of the rebel movement.

Jyn Erso resists the rebels at first, but she soon decides that she wants to help.

Mon Mothma at the Yavin 4 base.

Mon Mothma is the leader of the rebels. Her calm and patient attitude makes her the ideal person to unite various rebel groups.

Mon Mothma was a senator for many years. She believes in democracy and freedom. She opposed Palpatine being given more powers, even when most senators thought it was necessary. In the months before the formation of the Empire, Mon Mothma met secretly with Senator Bail Organa and several others. They prepared a plan of resistance to implement should Palpatine succeed in taking control.

To Mon Mothma's dismay, Palpatine appointed himself Emperor. Bail Organa pretended to remain loyal to the Empire, although he secretly sent money and ships to rebel groups. Mon Mothma, meanwhile, went into hiding, becoming the leader of the growing rebel movement.

Mon Mothma now travels among the various rebel headquarters. She aims to keep the different groups of rebels working together and ensure that all the top officers have their say.

Mon Mothma is determined to defeat the Empire and restore the democratic Republic, but she hopes to avoid drawing the entire galaxy into a terrible war.

Senator Bail Organa visits the rebel base on Yavin 4.

The rebel council is based on the planet moon Yavin 4. The base is concealed inside an ancient temple. The council is made up of military leaders—General Draven, Admiral Raddus, General Merrick, and General Dodonna—along with Mon Mothma and the senators who secretly support the rebel movement while appearing to remain loyal to the Empire.

Everyone on the council wants to free the galaxy from Imperial rule. However, they argue about everything from battlefield tactics to how

Mon
Mothma

General
Draven

to attract new rebel fighters. Mon Mothma tries to listen to everyone's opinion and come up with a plan that all can agree with.

When the council hears the rumor that the Empire has built a battle station capable of destroying a planet, it agrees to assemble a team to investigate. They select Captain Cassian Andor to lead the mission and ask Jyn Erso to accompany him, in the hope that they will be able to locate Saw Gerrera as well as Jyn's scientist father, Galen Erso.

Admiral
Raddus

General
Merrick

General
Dodonna

A Mon Calamari officer, Admiral Raddus was one of the first to join the rebel cause.

His homeworld, Mon Cala, risked the Emperor's wrath by openly opposing him. Mon Cala's stand against the Empire made the rebels far stronger. The Mon Calamari converted old transport ships into battleships that were tough enough to take on the Imperial fleet. These Mon Calamari ships now form the backbone of many rebel task forces.

Raddus is a careful tactician. He believes the way to achieve military victory is to calculate the odds—and never let emotions get in the way of decisions! Raddus and his fellow Mon Calamari officers encourage the rebels to keep moving between hidden bases. Instead of taking on the Empire in large-scale battles, the rebels should stage hit-and-run attacks, striking and then disappearing before the Empire can catch them.

When word reaches the rebels that the Empire's battle station is real, Raddus isn't sure what to do. What strategy could possibly work against a weapon able to destroy planets? However, Raddus puts his doubts aside and helps to plan the mission.

General Draven and General Merrick are veterans of many battles against the Empire.

Davits Draven dislikes politicians. He thinks they're good at talking but bad at fighting.

Rebel leader Mon Mothma wants to rescue Galen Erso and bring him to the Senate so he can reveal the truth about the Emperor's secret weapon. However, Draven thinks Erso knows too much. He secretly orders Cassian Andor to shoot Erso instead! Draven knows he will pay a price for disobeying orders, but believes it is his duty to keep his soldiers safe.

General Antoc Merrick is a skilled starfighter pilot who has worked with General Dodonna, Admiral Raddus, and veteran pilots such as Garven Dreis and Dutch Vander to figure out the best tactics to use when fighting the Empire.

Like Draven, Merrick sees protecting his pilots as his most important job and speaks up when he thinks those pilots' lives are at risk. Merrick despairs when he learns the Death Star is operational, but heads straight into battle, piloting an X-wing as Blue Leader, when his fellow rebels need him most.

Rogue One Team

Jyn Erso and Cassian Andor are unlikely partners on their mission to find Saw Gerrera on the moon Jedha. Both are skilled fighters, but their attitudes are very different. Jyn hasn't always cared about the rebel cause— she's been too busy trying to survive to worry about politics. Cassian, on the other hand, has fought against the Empire for his entire life, and feels a deep sense of duty to the rebel leaders.

Cassian
Andor

Jyn
Erso

Bodhi
Rook

Cassian thinks Jyn is selfish because she cares only about herself and not about the dangers that threaten the whole galaxy. To have any chance of stopping the Empire's evil plans, Jyn and Cassian will have to learn to trust one another.

Jyn and Cassian soon form a team—called Rogue One—with other rebels. The members of Rogue One must learn to work together, even though each of them has a different reason for choosing to join the mission.

Baze
Malbus

Chirrut
Îmwe

MEET THE TEAM

JYN ERSO

Newly recruited rebel. Eager to locate her father and end the threat of the Death Star.

Age: 21

Homeworld: Vallt

Skills: Trained to fight by Saw Gerrera

Weapons: Blaster, batons

CASSIAN ANDOR

Rebel Captain. Veteran soldier who has spent his life fighting against the Empire.

Age: 26

Homeworld: Fest

Skills: Spying, sabotage

Weapons: Blaster

K-2SO

Imperial droid reprogrammed as a rebel. Loyal to Cassian, distrustful of Jyn.

Years since construction: 12

World of construction: Vulpter

Skills: Fast runner, strong limbs, Imperial training

Weapons: None

BODHI ROOK

Defector from the Empire. Relieved to be following his conscience and fighting for galactic freedom.

Age: 25

Homeworld: Jedha

Skills: Computer expert, hacking skills, pilot skills

Weapons: None

BAZE MALBUS

Hot-headed warrior. Seeks revenge against the Empire.

Age: 53

Homeworld: Jedha

Skills: Trained in combat

Weapons: MWC-35c heavy repeating blaster

CHIRRUT ÎMWE

Spiritual warrior monk. Follows his heart and mind to do the right thing.

Age: 52

Homeworld: Jedha

Skills: Trained in the martial art of zama-shiwo

Weapons: Walking stick, lightbow

Life has been hard for Jyn Erso. When she was a girl, Orson Krennic's death troopers tracked her family down on Lah'mu. They captured her father, Galen, and forced him to return with them to Imperial territory. Jyn escaped with the help of an old family friend, the rebel Saw Gerrera. Saw taught Jyn to fight and kept her safe. However, they lost contact over the years.

Left alone, Jyn became a criminal, eventually winding up in an Imperial prison, until a group of rebels sent from Yavin 4 broke her out. The rebels claimed they needed Jyn's help to find her father and stop the Empire from building a planet-destroying superweapon.

Jyn was astonished to learn her father was still alive and frightened to discover that he might have helped create a terrifying weapon. She agrees to help the rebels, but is reluctant to do so. She hates the Empire, but life has taught her to trust no one. She feels like the rebels are merely using her, and she is certain they will abandon her once the mission is complete.

Despite his youth, Cassian Andor has spent much of his life fighting. As a boy growing up in the Outer Rim, Cassian was always drawn into battle against the growing influence of the Empire. When the Empire took over the galaxy completely, Cassian kept fighting, and was soon recruited to the rebel cause.

Cassian is now a captain in Rebel Intelligence and a veteran of many missions. He is skilled at spying, enemy sabotage, and assassination, and some of his missions have required him to do terrible things. Cassian gets angry when people criticize the rebels' actions without understanding the difficult choices that must often be made during the heat of a battle.

Cassian is a respected captain who also respects his own superiors. He wants to do the job right and get the job done. Those under his command are reassured to have a leader who is calm under pressure and an experienced soldier, familiar with stealthy and dangerous missions.

Captain Andor is the perfect choice to lead the dangerous mission to Jedha.

Although K-2SO began his existence as an Imperial droid, he was reprogrammed by Cassian and now serves the rebels.

The hulking droid stands more than two meters tall. He is clad in black metal with a skull-like head, a massive chest, and long limbs.

This KX-model enforcer droid was built to provide security in Imperial facilities. KX droids interview visitors and escort them to meetings, but they can also defend Imperial personnel or attack intruders. Their long, ball-jointed legs make them fast runners, and their long arms and strong hands can restrain enemies—or attack them until they surrender.

K-2SO accompanied the rebel soldiers who rescued Jyn Erso from prison. The security droid then traveled to Jedha with Cassian and Jyn. K-2SO wasn't programmed for politeness, and bluntly tells Jyn that he thinks it is a bad idea to take her on the mission.

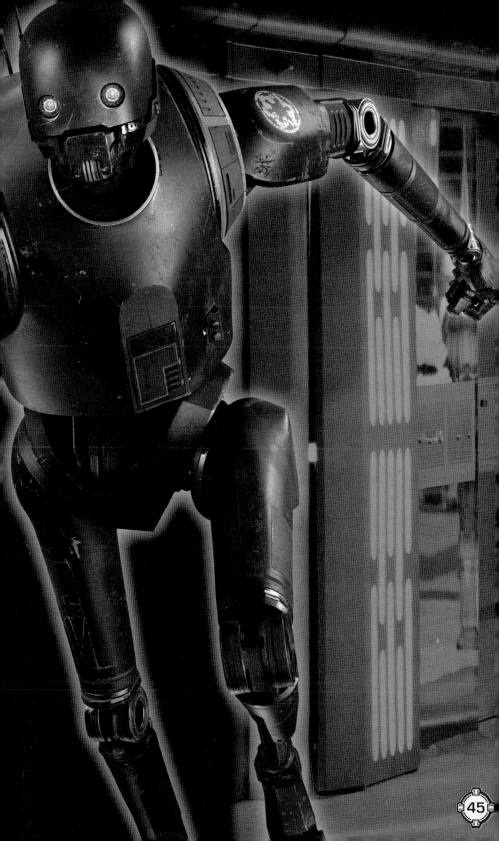

KEEN SENSORS
Photoreceptors can process more than human eyes. Hearing is far better than that of most organic beings.

TOUGH CUSTOMER
Heavy, reinforced chest armor can withstand direct impacts from blaster bolts. K-2SO can absorb damage while attacking targets or shielding allies.

ON ALERT
Like many security droids, K-2SO is programmed to search for signs of intruders.

BUILT FOR SPEED
Mechanical components in thighs drive K-2SO's long legs, working together with powerful motors and sturdy suspension.

ATHLETIC DROID
K-2SO's complex balance systems allow him to change direction with surprising speed and grace.

RUNNING MACHINE
Wide, flat feet support K-2SO's weight, even on soft or uneven terrain.

K-2SO

REBEL UPGRADES
Cassian Andor bypassed K-2SO's behavioral and security programming, making him loyal to the rebels.

MISTAKEN IDENTITY
Imperial symbol remains on shoulder, so the KX droid can be used to infiltrate Imperial bases.

SENSE OF SMELL
Chest-mounted olfactory sensors give K-2SO a keen sense of smell.

NO LIMITS
As a security droid, K-2SO lacks the usual safeguards that prevent him from harming organic beings.

VERSATILE
K-2SO is programmed to use many tools and can carry far heavier loads than a typical human can.

LISTENING POST
K-2SO's built-in communications booster lets him scan frequencies used by Imperials.

HIDDEN TOOL
K-2SO's hands conceal hidden data spikes for computer access.

BALANCING ACT
Sensors in legs constantly monitor body position. Leg mechanisms keep K-2SO upright, balancing against his bulky upper body.

SPECIFICATIONS

Chirrut Îmwe is a monk from the moon Jedha. It would be easy to dismiss Chirrut as one of the many beggars in Jedha's Holy City, but that would be a mistake. Despite being blind, Chirrut is a deadly warrior.

Chirrut is a member of the Guardians of the Whills, a group of warrior monks who have defended the mysterious Temple of the Kyber on Jedha for millennia. He uses his walking stick as a deadly weapon. He also carries a concealed lightbow, which he can aim accurately despite his blindness. Chirrut practices an ancient martial art known as zama-shiwo. It allows him to use his other senses to read his environment.

While Cassian and Jyn wait to make contact with Saw Gerrera's men outside the Temple, they are attacked by stormtroopers. Chirrut and his friend Baze Malbus jump to their aid.

Chirrut believes that the ancient energy field called the Force connects all living things. He believes that the Force has brought him into contact with Cassian and Jyn, so he dedicates himself to helping them.

Baze Malbus was once a Guardian of the Whills, serving alongside his friend Chirrut Îmwe. But he has now shed the order's robes and wears combat armor instead. The Empire's occupation of Jedha has left Baze deeply angry.

He is determined to make the stormtroopers pay for what the Empire has done.

Baze's MWC-35c heavy repeating blaster packs the destructive power of five ordinary blasters. A flexible, reinforced charging cord connects the barrel with a power cell carried in a backpack. Baze can clear an entire battlefield with a devastating storm of laser fire.

Baze and Chirrut are close friends, but couldn't be more different. Baze is hot-tempered while Chirrut is calm and quiet, and Baze rolls his eyes when his friend quotes spiritual teachings. Though he'd never admit it, Baze appreciates that Chirrut always looks after him. After an Imperial attack devastates Jedha, the old friends remain side by side, fighting together for the rebel cause.

Bodhi Rook grew up on Jedha. He remembers when the planet was beautiful, before the Empire destroyed it by mining for kyber crystals and sent stormtroopers to occupy Jedha's Holy City. Bodhi always loved to fly, so he joined the Empire to become a pilot. He has flown many shipments of kyber crystals from Jedha to the Imperial research facility on Eadu. Bodhi always hated what the Empire did to Jedha, but felt he was powerless to change things, until he met scientist Galen Erso. Erso convinced Bodhi to listen to his conscience, and persuaded him to defect from the Empire. Galen sent Bodhi to Saw Gerrera with a message, informing Saw that the Imperials are secretly building a devastating weapon.

When Cassian and Jyn make contact with Saw, Bodhi joins the rebels' fight against the Empire. Bodhi is nervous about committing himself to the rebel cause, but Galen has taught him to listen to his heart. He now wants to do everything he can to stop the Empire's dreaded weapon from threatening freedom in the galaxy.

Bodhi's hacking skills are very useful. He carries a cable to hack into Imperial systems.

As a young man, Saw Gerrera fought against the armies that invaded his homeworld of Onderon. Saw continued his fight against the Empire, and over the years his war became an intensely personal one. He thinks that brutal tactics are necessary to hurt the Empire, an extreme attitude that has caused the other rebel groups to break ties with Saw's group.

Saw helped Galen Erso and his wife escape from the Empire years ago, and he rescued their daughter Jyn when Director Krennic tracked the family down on Lah'mu. Saw raised Jyn and taught her to fight. He cared for her as if she were his daughter.

Years later, Saw is surprised when an Imperial defector named Bodhi Rook tracks him down on Jedha, with a message from Galen. Saw is much older now, and scarred by many injuries, but he is ready for a final showdown with the Empire.

Imperial Military

When the Clone Wars ended, most people expected the Republic to dismantle its armies of clone troopers and scrap its fleets of warships. Instead, the Republic became the Empire, and the vast military force it had built grew even larger.

Imperial Star Destroyers and TIE fighters darkened the skies of worlds in the Outer Rim, while huge walking machines and stormtroopers destroyed any opposition on the ground. These faceless soldiers became a symbol of the Empire's power, battling its enemies and seeking out any sign of resistance to Emperor Palpatine's rule.

Gigantic Star Destroyers are an intimidating sight.

Stormtroopers and shoretroopers prepare to embark on a mission.

Stormtroopers are the most common sign of enforcement on planets occupied by the Empire, but specialized units can also be seen from time to time. Lightly armored tank troopers patrol cities, scout troopers undertake reconnaissance missions, and elite stormtrooper squads, such as death troopers, guard important Imperial officers. Rumor has it that other squads of specially trained soldiers serve in hostile environments and pursue top-secret missions for their Emperor.

The All Terrain Armored Cargo Transport (AT-ACT) is an imposing four-legged walking machine. It is a variant of the Empire's better-known AT-AT walker, but designed to carry cargo instead of troops.

Traditional Imperial cargo transports are often a target for pirates hoping to steal weapons, or rebels looking to destroy military equipment. By adapting a military vehicle to serve as a cargo transport, the Empire solved this problem. The AT-ACT's weapons are as devastating as those of an AT-AT, which makes enemies think twice before launching an attack.

A key role of the AT-ACT has been to safely transport shipments of kyber crystals. These precious crystals are an essential resource for use in the construction of the Death Star.

AT-ACTs are deployed to defend the Imperial base on Scarif.

Clad in bright white armor, stormtroopers are the foot soldiers of the Empire.

The Empire fills its armies with graduates from purpose-built Imperial Academies. Academy recruits are often youngsters who are forced into the training program, although some recruits volunteer as well. Stormtrooper training is intense, with the goal of producing large numbers of ruthless, obedient troopers. Stormtroopers wear a black body glove beneath their armor, which protects them from harsh environments and the vacuum of deep space. Their white armor plates can withstand hits from projectiles and glancing blows from blaster bolts.

Stormtroopers storm the beach on the planet Scarif.

Typical stormtrooper units are armed with lightweight E-11 blasters. These offer deadly firepower and excellent range. For missions where longer-range combat is likely, stormtroopers use DLT-19 rifles. All troopers carry thermal detonators on their utility belts.

Stormtrooper armor is quite bulky, so scout and reconnaissance units often wear partial armor to improve their mobility and vision. Extended operations in hostile environments may require specialized gear. Sometimes, specialist units, trained for certain environments, will be sent in place of standard stormtrooper units.

Death troopers are members of an elite stormtrooper unit that serves Imperial Intelligence and other key officials. They act as bodyguards and enforcers for top officers, including Director Krennic. Death troopers' glossy black armor is superior to regular stormtrooper armor. It is treated with an advanced coating that makes it hard for sensors to detect. Their helmets have sophisticated antennas, which give death troopers excellent awareness of the battlefield. Their E-11D blaster rifles have been modified to give increased firepower over greater distances. Death troopers are ideal for stealth missions: they can slip through a target's defenses, attack with speed and precision, and withdraw as quickly as they arrive.

Only the most skilled stormtrooper cadets can become death troopers. They train in secret camps on the Imperial fortress world of Scarif, learning advanced combat tactics. As part of this training, death troopers are brainwashed into showing absolute loyalty to the high-ranking officers that they will protect and serve.

Death troopers are a fearsome sight that is often more than enough to make an enemy surrender.

Shoretroopers are a specialist stormtrooper unit trained to patrol shorelines and beach environments. The white sands, warm seas, and green jungles of the planet Scarif make it seem like a tropical paradise. Look closer, however, and you'll find that this Outer Rim planet is dotted with Imperial facilities.

Shoretroopers defend the Imperial base on Scarif, protecting its store of kyber crystals.

Scarif's beaches and jungles are patrolled by shoretroopers—a nickname derived from the beige coloring of their armor and their brown fatigues. Like death trooper helmets, shoretrooper helmets have viewplates to detect movement and powerful comlinks for long-range communication. Shoretroopers wear lightweight, flexible armor to make them less clumsy in combat and prevent them from becoming exhausted in Scarif's heat.

Despite Scarif's strong defenses, patrolling this planet is no easy mission. The Empire maintains high security at all times, keeping shoretroopers and other units alert with nonstop drills and training exercises. The planet's defenders are prepared for any breach or attack.

Tank troopers are a common sight in the occupied Holy City of Jedha. Imperial forces on Jedha rely on combat assault tanks, speeder bikes, and AT-ST scout walkers to keep the peace.

The combat assault tanks are fast and bristle with weapons—their heavy cannons can reduce a stone building to rubble in minutes. The tanks are effective on many rebellious worlds, but they have disadvantages on Jedha. The Holy City's streets are extremely narrow, and are often filled with people. Tank commanders often find they can't fit down an alleyway, or that they cannot chase a fugitive through a crowd.

Tank trooper units wear partial armor instead of the bulkier gear worn by regular stormtroopers. They sacrifice full-body protection to gain speed and ease of movement to help fight on Jedha's urban battlefields. When not aboard their assault vehicles, tank troopers are sent out on raids and patrol missions in the winding, narrow streets of the Holy City. Like all stormtroopers, they are well-equipped, well-trained, and fully loyal to the Imperial cause.

Fast and lethal, TIE fighters are the frontline starfighters of the Empire. Their speed comes from a combination of powerful twin ion engines and lightweight hull armor. TIEs lack defensive shields, but their pilots regard their fighters' vulnerability as a point of pride. They survive by relying on their skill and nerve to outfly opponents.

When flying in planetary atmospheres, air resistance slows down standard TIEs and makes them less maneuverable. To counter this weakness, the Empire has developed a variant fighter—the TIE striker.

TIE strikers are more streamlined than regular TIEs, with elongated cockpits and dagger-shaped wings that can fold up or down. This makes them faster and more maneuverable, while their weapons are every bit as powerful. The Empire uses TIE strikers for planetary missions, flying above worlds such as Jedha and Scarif.

TIE pilots who survive their training often specialize either in deep-space missions or atmospheric duty. TIE pilots who fly "in the black" (in space) are nicknamed vac-heads, while pilots who fly "in the blue" (in planetary atmospheres) are called ground-hogs. These two groups of pilots are fierce rivals.

THE DEATH STAR
The Empire's battle station, taking
shape above the planet Scarif,
is the size of a small moon and
the largest weapon known
in galactic history.

Death Star
Diameter: 160 km (99 miles)

SCALE OF THE EMPIRE

The Empire's war fleets include everything from
small single-man starfighters to massive battleships
that are kilometers in length. All are strong symbols
of the Emperor's power over the galaxy's people.

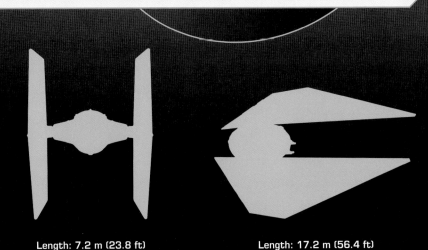

Length: 7.2 m (23.8 ft)

Length: 17.2 m (56.4 ft)

TIE FIGHTER
The standard starfighter of the
Empire, the TIE is speedy and
maneuverable, but lacks shields
and thick, protective hull armor.

TIE STRIKER
A new addition to the Empire's
starfighter ranks, the TIE striker
is designed for missions in
planetary atmospheres.

Imperial Star Destroyer

TIE fighter
Length: 7.2 m (23.8 ft)

Imperial Star Destroyer
Length: 1.6 km (1 mile)

IMPERIAL STAR DESTROYERS

These huge, dagger-shaped warships are the
backbone of the Imperial starfleet. They are fast
enough to run down enemy ships and powerful
enough to rip them apart with their turbolasers.

Length: 35.5 m (116.4 ft)

Length: 14.4 m (47.2 ft)

SCARIF MINING TRANSPORT

The Imperial army relies on
transports to carry equipment
and resources, such as kyber
crystals, swiftly and safely.

KRENNIC'S SHUTTLE

Fitted with imposing wings,
Delta-class T-3C shuttles protect
high-ranking Imperials, such as
Krennic, on important missions.

Rebel Military

The small groups of rebels that are spread across the galaxy cannot match the Empire's huge military.

The rebels fight with scavenged and stolen starships and use older gear and weapons. Despite these shortcomings, the rebels often prove themselves more than a match for the Empire in battle. How is this possible?

One reason is that the rebel movement gets secret support from senators who find a way to divert weapons, supplies, and sometimes even starships from the Empire to the rebels' hidden bases. The battlefields of the Clone Wars are still littered with ground vehicles and gear that rebels can salvage, fix up, and even improve.

The rebels are also superbly trained. Many of their top officers served the Empire before listening to their consciences and finding a new allegiance.

Captain Cassian Andor is loyal to the rebel cause.

Some rebels, such as Saw Gerrera and Cassian Andor, have been soldiers since they were young.

Most importantly of all, the rebels all believe passionately in their cause, pledging to sacrifice even their lives if that's what is needed to defeat the Empire once and for all.

Rebels often modify and improve their ships and equipment.

Rebels and droids work together to keep the Rebellion running.

Like the Empire, the rebels rely on droids to take care of an enormous number of duties. Droids are a common sight at rebel bases across the galaxy, and often risk their mechanical existences alongside soldiers and pilots.

At the Yavin 4 base, droids do everything from maintaining starfighters to assisting the movement's leaders with communications and strategy. Rebel pilots rely more heavily than Imperial pilots on assistance from droids: both X-wings and Y-wings have droid sockets for astromechs, who communicate constantly with pilots while handling repairs, improving systems, and performing hyperspace calculations.

Rebel technicians give droids memory wipes when necessary to preserve security, but some mechanicals are spared this treatment. Sometimes a droid's master sees behavioral quirks as personality traits to be respected, instead of programming errors to be deleted. Older-model droids continue to serve the rebel cause despite being regarded as outdated. And while the Empire hardly ever grants droids their freedom, the rebel ranks include a number of free droids who now serve voluntarily.

Astromech droid
R2-BHD

GNK power
droid

Astromech
droid R3-S1

MISSION REPORT

1 JEDHA RENDEZVOUS

OBJECTIVE: Locate Saw Gerrera on Jedha. Retrieve intel about the upcoming Imperial weapons test.
OUTCOME: Mission success.

2 TARGET ON EADU

OBJECTIVE: Locate Galen Erso, lead scientist on the Imperial weapon project. Jyn to identify him.
OUTCOME: Mission success.
NOTE: Jyn and Cassian now accompanied by Bodhi Rook, Baze Malbus, and Chirrut Îmwe.

What began as a simple recon and rescue mission has turned into something much more dangerous. After learning that the Death Star plans are hidden on Scarif, Jyn and Cassian ignore the orders of their rebel leaders to remain at base. Instead, they travel to the fortress planet of Scarif, intent on stealing the Death Star plans.

3 YAVIN 4 DEBRIEF

OBJECTIVE: Return to Yavin 4 to regroup with rebel council.

OUTCOME: Rebel council decides to take no further action on this matter.

WARNING! Cassian, Jyn, and team defy orders and head for Scarif, hoping to locate Death Star plans.

4 SCARIF HEIST

OBJECTIVE: Sneak past Imperial forces on Scarif and locate the secret Death Star plans.

OUTCOME: Rebel presence detected on Scarif. Rogue One team come under heavy Imperial attack.

An experienced soldier in the rebels' Special Forces, Infiltrator Sergeant Ruescott Melshi is a good friend of Cassian's. When Cassian asks Melshi to lead a group of SpecForces soldiers into the battle on Scarif, Melshi doesn't hesitate. Melshi hastily puts together a team of SpecForces commandos—including Lieutenant Sefla, Corporal Restak, and the warrior Pao—to assist the Rogue One team.

Melshi leads his soldiers through the jungles of Scarif.

Melshi realizes that the Imperial forces on Scarif are far more numerous than his small team of soldiers. His plan is for the rebels to attack with such force and noise that they appear more powerful than they really are.

Sergeant Melshi makes it clear to his soldiers that the mission is voluntary—in fact, those who join are disobeying orders and could find themselves in considerable trouble. But then the galaxy is already in trouble, isn't it? Melshi is grateful when more than a dozen of his commandos volunteer to join him.

A SpecForces warrior, Paodok'Draba'Takat—Pao for short—is an amphibious Drabata from the planet Pipada. He hates the Empire for what it has done to his homeworld, and he eagerly answers Melshi's call to join the Rogue One mission. Pao is trained to handle explosives, a skill he uses as the commandos cause chaos in the jungles of Scarif.

Like all Drabata, Pao has big lungs and powerful diaphragm muscles, which let him hold his breath for a long time. He also has a booming voice. On Scarif, he charges into battle with a Drabatese war cry of "Sa'kalla!"

Another SpecForces soldier, Bistan is an Iakaru warrior. He serves as a door gunner on the commandos' U-wing as it makes the perilous descent to the surface of Scarif. Like all rebel commandos, Bistan endured months of demanding physical and tactical training before he was granted a spot in SpecForces. He learned to fight with numerous weapons in various dangerous conditions. He puts his training to good use during the mission, tirelessly firing away at Scarif's Imperial defenders with his blaster.

The T-65 X-wing is the rebel movement's top starfighter. It has evolved from older starfighters such as the Z-95 and the ARC-170. With its powerful engines, tough shields and armor, and deadly weapons, it is a versatile craft that can hold its own battling with TIEs or slugging it out with warships.

Harb
Binli

Broan
Danurs

Zal
Dinnes

Despite its advanced capabilities, the X-wing is relatively simple to fly, responding quickly and easily to a pilot's commands. This allows the rebels to train gifted pilots quickly, getting them behind the stick of an X-wing and into combat in hours instead of weeks.

The X-wing pilots of Yavin 4's rebel base pride themselves on their ability to succeed at any mission thrown their way. One of the rebels' many frustrations is that they have more pilots than starfighters. They can only send up as many X-wings as their skilled maintenance crews can prepare for a mission.

The rebels mainly use the sturdy UT-60D gunship transport, or U-wing, as a troop transport. This craft is built by the same manufacturer as the X-wing. It has powerful front-mounted cannons and a quartet of rear-mounted engines that let the U-wing avoid enemy fire, swoop down to battlefields, and then quickly lift off once its passengers are clear.

U-wing pilots need nerves of steel and the ability to stay calm. Every instinct tells starfighter pilots to keep moving rather than sit still and risk a storm of laser fire raining down on them.

U-wing pilots have no choice but to wait until the troops they are carrying have disembarked before they can take flight.

As a veteran U-wing pilot himself, rebel leader General Merrick knows what a tough job the pilots have. He considers it his duty to look after all the pilots of the rebel fleet. U-wings ferry Jyn and Cassian from Yavin 4 to Jedha. From there, they take them to Eadu to search for Galen Erso, and later take part in the Battle of Scarif.

General Merrick commands all the starfighter pilots from the Yavin 4 base.

The rebels' stolen ship doesn't last long on Scarif.

The Battle of Scarif begins as a hastily planned raid by rebels disobeying orders and becomes a fight to preserve freedom in the galaxy. Cassian and Jyn lead their team—team Rogue One—with a group of rebel soldiers, to Scarif on a desperate mission: find the Death Star plans and deliver them into the hands of the rebel council.

Baze and Chirrut target Imperial troopers, allowing Jyn and Cassian to infiltrate the Imperial base. They hope to upload the plans to their stolen Imperial cargo ship, which Bodhi will fly to safety.

Rebel fighters strike hard at Imperial troops.

It is a desperate gamble, but the team isn't alone: Yavin 4's rebels send a task force of ships and starfighters to Scarif to help. Rebel soldiers battle Imperial vehicles on the beach as X-wings and TIEs duel overhead, buying time for the rebel team. When the mission starts to go wrong—as missions so often do—Jyn frantically takes the Death Star plans to a communications tower, hoping to transmit them from there.

The Battle of Scarif sees many brave rebels risk their lives. The Empire's TIE fighters and Star Destroyers battle the rebels' X-wings, Y-wings, and U-wings in space, while the rebel soldiers on the shores of Scarif are pinned down by laser fire from AT-ACTs and Imperial forces.

Whether Jyn and the rebels win or lose this battle, the Death Star remains a threat to peaceful planets everywhere. Ruthless leaders, such as Grand Moff Tarkin and Darth Vader will still seek to hunt down and destroy the rebels.

However, the threat of the Death Star causes a hugely important change. It finally convinces the feuding groups of rebels to put aside their differences and unite as a true alliance fighting for freedom. Now, with the glimmer of hope that they might be able to destroy the Death Star, the Rebel Alliance has a chance to win an even bigger victory, bringing a new hope to the galaxy.

Jyn inspires her fellow rebels to unite against the threat of the Empire. She hopes the Force will be with them all.

Quiz

1. Which Imperial officer is the Director of Advanced Weapons Research?

2. What is the name of Jyn Erso's mother?

3. Who rescued Jyn from an Imperial attack on Lah'mu?

4. What are Director Krennic's elite, black-armored stormtroopers called?

5. What is the name of the pilot who brings Galen Erso's message to Saw Gerrera?

6. Who is the leader of the rebel movement?

7. What is the homeworld of Admiral Raddus?

8. What powers the Death Star's superlaser?

9. Who gives secret orders to Cassian Andor?

10. What planet is the Temple of the Kyber found on?

11. What martial art does Chirrut Îmwe practice?

12. What weapon does Baze Malbus use?

13. What TIE model is designed for use in planetary atmospheres?

14. On what planet are the Death Star plans?

15. To which elite rebel battle unit does Sergeant Melshi belong?

Answers on page 96

Glossary

amphibious
Able to live on land and in water.

Clone Wars
A war between the Republic and its enemies that ended with the Republic becoming the Empire.

clone troopers
Genetically identical humans who fought for the Republic in the Clone Wars.

defector
A person who abandons his or her allegiance to a group to support a different one.

democracy
A system of government that is fair and just.

Empire
The current government of the galaxy, led by Emperor Palpatine and ruled using force.

Force
A mystical energy that flows through all living things.

fugitive
Someone who is running away.

Guardians of the Whills
A mysterious group of warrior monks who protect the Temple of the Kyber.

infiltrate
To enter a place secretly.

intent
Determined to do something.

Jedi Knights
Guardians of the Republic, who were mostly wiped out at the end of the Clone Wars.

kyber crystal
A crystal that channels energy. Once used to power lightsabers and now a crucial part of the Death Star's superlaser.

lightbow
A handheld weapon, traditional to Jedha, that's used by Chirrut Îmwe.

occupied
Taken over by military force.

Outer Rim Territories
    The outermost part of the galaxy, now being brought under control of the Empire.

photoreceptors
    Artificial eyes used by droids.

pioneering
    Creating new ideas.

quadanium
    A durable metal.

rebel council
    A group that makes decisions for the rebel movement.

rebels
    A collection of loosely allied groups seeking to overthrow the Empire and restore the Republic.

reconnaissance
    Finding out information about a location or enemy before a mission begins.

Republic
    The former government of the galaxy, which became the Empire.

Senate
    A branch of the Imperial government made up of senators—representatives of the galaxy's planets.

superlaser
    The primary weapon of the Death Star, powered by kyber crystals and able to destroy a planet.

tactician
    Someone who is good at making plans.

Temple of the Kyber
    An ancient, mystical temple on the moon Jedha.

tractor beam
    A device that bends gravity to direct energy in a certain direction.

urban
    A city or town landscape.

veteran
    A person who is experienced in battle.

versatile
    Something that has many uses.

Guide for Parents

This book is part of an exciting four-level reading series for children, developing the habit of reading widely for both pleasure and information. These chapter books have a compelling main narrative to suit your child's reading ability. Each book is designed to develop your child's reading skills, fluency, grammar awareness, and comprehension in order to build confidence and engagement when reading.

Ready for a *Level 4* book

YOUR CHILD SHOULD

- be able to read most words without needing to stop and break them down into sound parts.
- read smoothly, in phrases and with expression. By this level, your child will be mostly reading silently.
- self-correct when some word or sentence doesn't sound right.

A VALUABLE AND SHARED READING EXPERIENCE

For some children, text reading, particularly nonfiction, requires much effort, but adult participation can make this both fun and easier. So here are a few tips on how to use this book with your child.

TIP 1 Check out the contents together before your child begins:

- invite your child to check the back cover text, contents page, and layout of the book and comment on it.
- ask your child to make predictions about the story.
- talk about the information your child might want to find out.

TIP 2 Encourage fluent and flexible reading:

- support your child to read in fluent, expressive phrases, making full use of punctuation and thinking about the meaning.

- encourage your child to slow down and check information where appropriate.

TIP 3 Indicators that your child is reading for meaning:

- your child will be responding to the text if he/she is self-correcting and varying his/her voice.

- your child will want to talk about what he/she is reading or is eager to turn the page to find out what will happen next.

TIP 4 Share and discuss:

- encourage your child to recall specific details after each chapter.

- provide opportunities for your child to pick out interesting words and discuss what they mean.

- discuss how the author captures the reader's interest, or how effective the nonfiction layouts are.

- ask questions about the text. These help develop comprehension skills and awareness of the language used.

A FEW ADDITIONAL TIPS

- Read to your child regularly to demonstrate fluency, phrasing, and expression; to find out or check information; and for sharing enjoyment.

- Encourage your child to reread favorite texts to increase reading confidence and fluency.

- Check that your child is reading a range of different types of material, such as poems, jokes, and following instructions.

Index

Admiral Raddus 30–33, 35

AT-ACT 58, 88

Baze Malbus 37, 39, 48, 50–51, 76, 86

Bistan 81

Bodhi Rook 17, 26–27, 36, 39, 52–54, 76, 86

Cassian Andor 26, 31, 34, 36–38, 43–44, 47–49, 53, 72–73, 76–78, 85–86

Chirrut Îmwe 37, 39, 48–51, 76, 86

Clone Wars 4, 14, 56, 72

Darth Vader 9–11, 15, 88

Death Star 5–9, 11, 13–23, 35, 38, 58, 70, 77, 86–88

death trooper 13, 17, 40, 57, 62–63, 65

droid 38, 44, 46–47, 74–75

Eadu 7, 13, 17, 19, 52, 76, 85

Emperor 5, 8–10, 13–15, 20, 29, 32, 34, 56–57, 70 see also Palpatine

Galen Erso 6–7, 13–17, 19, 21, 27, 31, 34, 40, 53–54, 76, 85

General Dodonna 30–31, 35

General Draven 30, 34–35

General Merrick 30–31, 34–35, 85

Grand Moff Tarkin 9, 13, 20–21, 88

Jedha 5, 7, 26, 36, 39, 43–44, 48, 50–52, 54, 67, 69, 76, 85

Jedi 4–5, 11, 14–15

Jyn Erso 14–17, 27, 31, 36–38, 40, 44, 48–49, 53–54, 76–77, 85–88

K-2SO 36, 38, 44, 46–47

kyber crystals 19–20, 22, 52, 58, 64, 71

Lah'mu 6, 15–17, 40, 54

Lyra Erso 14, 16–17

Mon Mothma 25, 28–31, 34

Orson Krennic 7, 9, 13–21, 40, 54, 62, 71

Palpatine 4–5, 8–9, 14, 28–29, 56 see also Emperor

Pao 78, 80

rebel council 30–31, 77, 86

Republic 4, 14, 29, 56

Rogue One 14, 36–37, 77–78, 80, 86

Saw Gerrera 7, 15, 17, 26–27, 31, 36, 38, 40, 48, 53–54, 73, 76

Scarif 7, 15, 58, 61, 63–65, 69–71, 77–81, 85–88

Sergeant Melshi 78–80

shoretrooper 57, 64–65

Star Destroyer 56, 71, 88

stormtrooper 8, 13, 26, 48, 51–52, 56–57, 60–64, 67

tank trooper 57, 67

TIE fighter 23, 56, 68–71, 82, 87–88

TIE striker 68–70

U-wing 81, 84–85, 88

X-wing 35, 74, 82–84, 87–88

Yavin 4 6, 27–30, 40, 74, 77, 83, 85, 87